FROM THE LIBRARY OF

Peter Beach

Frederic
REMINGTON
Artist on Horseback

Frederic
REMINGTON
ARTIST ON HORSEBACK

by LaVere Anderson

GARRARD PUBLISHING COMPANY
Champaign, Illinois

TO
CAL, DAN, AND POLLY
WHO LIVE IN THE WEST THAT
FREDERIC REMINGTON
PAINTED SO BEAUTIFULLY

Picture Credits:

Art Division, New York Public Library: p. 1, 42, 56, 59 (all),
80, 87, 96 (both), 99, 110, 116, 129

Thomas Gilcrease Institute, Tulsa, Oklahoma: p. 141

The Kansas State Historical Society, Topeka, Kansas: p. 54

Remington Art Memorial Museum, Ogdensburg, New York: p. 2, 6, 12,
18, 23, 28, 32, 49, 50, 51, 52, 66, 69, 72, 78, 92, 101, 102,
103, 104, 125, 134, 146

Copyright © 1971 by LaVere Anderson

All rights reserved. Manufactured in the U.S.A.

Standard Book Number: 8116-4509-6

Library of Congress Catalog Card Number: 73-127181

Contents

1. A Game of Indians 7
2. News from Far Places 17
3. Art and Football 26
4. The Trail West 34
5. Big Land, Big Sky 40
6. In the Saddle 48
7. A Ranch in Kansas 62
8. Apache Land 73
9. Pictures for Sale 82
10. Success Story 91
11. Last of the Indian Wars 107
12. Beauty in Bronze 118
13. The Charge at San Juan Hill 127
14. An Artist's Life 131
15. End of the Trail 140
    Index 150

Young Frederic Remington and his mother, Clara Remington, posed for this early photograph.

1. A Game of Indians

"Frederic, you may read the next line of the exercise," Master Jason said.

The schoolmaster peered through his spectacles at a sandy-haired boy of nine sitting in the third row of desks. It was October 1870, in the little town of Canton, New York. A pale autumn sun shone through the schoolroom windows and on the sandy-colored head bent low over a book.

"Frederic!" Master Jason said again, then loudly, "FREDERIC REMINGTON!"

Still the boy did not look up.

Every child in the room turned to stare as the master walked swiftly to Fred's desk. The boy was busily drawing a picture on the margin of a page in his reader. The teacher's long finger poked Fred's shoulder. Startled, Fred raised his head.

His round face turned fiery red as he realized what had happened. He'd been caught not paying attention—and he'd marked up his book!

"I—sir, I—" he began. Then suddenly he blurted out the thing that really worried him. "I can't get the legs right! They're too big." He pointed to his drawing. It showed an Indian with his scalping knife held high above a victim.

The master gazed down at the drawing. It was a child's simple sketch, yet there was a look of life about it.

"Um—" he said. He liked boys. Still, he also liked his scholars to pay attention in class. How else could he teach them to read and spell and figure sums? So he made his voice stern as he said, "You will now read the fourth line of the exercise."

Fred stood up and read haltingly: "He 'tended dav-ine ser-vus reg-larly."

The master frowned. "You did not sound your

vowels. 'He *a*ttended d*i*vine serv*i*ce reg*u*larly.' You will stay after school and write the sentence twenty times, and underline every vowel."

A titter ran through the class, led by a boy called Badger. It wasn't his name but he deserved it because he badgered and bullied the smaller boys.

Fred glared at Badger, but Badger only grinned and made a face at him.

After school Fred copied the sentence while the teacher sat waiting at his big desk. It did not occur to Fred that Master Jason was having to stay after school, too. At last Fred finished and took his work to the desk.

The schoolmaster nodded. "Hereafter you will remember to sound your vowels, Frederic," he said. "Give me your reader."

Now he was in for it! the boy thought. Master Jason hadn't forgotten that he'd marked up his book.

The master opened the reader and looked again at the picture of the Indian. "Um—yes. The legs are a little too big," he said.

He handed Fred a folded sheet of heavy paper. When Fred opened it he saw it was a large advertising broadside. There was printing on the front but the back was clean and white.

"Cut it into smaller sheets and tack them to a thin board," Master Jason said. "It will make a better sketch pad than your schoolbooks."

"Thank you, sir!" the astonished boy exclaimed. "I—I'll sound my vowels!" He ran out the door hugging the precious paper to his chest. He had never had such smooth white paper before. He'd had only rough, oatmeal-gray pencil tablets that cost two pennies at the general store. There were stacks of them in his desk at home, all filled with sketches he had made of soldiers and Indians, but mostly of horses.

To Fred Remington's eyes, nothing else in the world was so beautiful as a horse. He had been drawing horses ever since his fingers were big enough to hold a pencil.

Now through the streets of Canton he raced. If he hurried there would be time to make his sketch pad before supper.

Fred had lived in the little college town all his life. Canton was near the Canadian border and a few miles from the St. Lawrence River. There were pleasant woods nearby where a boy could ride his pony, and clear sweet streams in which to swim and fish. There were trees to climb and trails to hike and small game to hunt. In winter the snow piled high and ponds froze, perfect for sledding and skating.

Fred enjoyed the outdoor life almost as much as he liked to draw. His father encouraged him in both. Colonel Seth P. Remington published a Canton newspaper, the *St. Lawrence Plaindealer*, but he had been a hard-riding cavalry officer during the Civil War. On his return he had taught his son, and only child, to ride well. Fred and his pony knew every twisting trail through the woods.

Fred's mother did not always understand her active, high-spirited son. She worried when Fred was the first Canton boy to dive into the cold streams in the spring and last to leave them in the fall. Every kind of sport appealed to him, and he never ran away from a fistfight.

Colonel Remington, Fred's
father, was the publisher
of Canton's *St. Lawrence
Plaindealer.*

When he reached home Fred collected a ham-
mer, tacks, and his mother's big sewing scissors
and set out again—this time for his uncle's stable.
Since the uncle no longer kept horses, he let Fred
have a "studio" in the stable. Fred often borrowed
the neighbors' carriage horses and took them to
the studio to study and sketch them.

In the big barn, with its dusty smell of old hay
and cobwebs, the boy sat on the floor cutting his

sheet of paper. Suddenly a figure stood at the open door.

"What you doing? Cutting paper dolls?" sneered Badger.

Fred laid his scissors on the floor and picked up his papers. You couldn't work with Badger around.

Badger strolled into the barn. He spied some feathers that Fred had nailed to a wooden post. "What's that?" Badger demanded.

"Eagle feathers," Fred said, "like the Indian braves wear."

Badger snickered. "They're nothing but the tail feathers of an old rooster. You don't know anything about eagles or Indians."

"I do, too," Fred cried. "Besides, they *look* like eagle feathers."

"Wa-hoo!" Badger whooped suddenly. "I'm an Indian on the warpath and I'm capturing you." He grabbed at Fred. Fred dodged. Fred was strong and big for his age, but Badger was older and bigger. Badger jerked the papers from Fred, threw them on the ground and stamped on them.

For a second Fred stood stricken. Then like a fury he flew at the older boy, pummeling him with tight fists. Taken by surprise, Badger stumbled and fell. Fred was astride him instantly. Fred saw the scissors lying on the floor. Inspiration seized him. He snatched up the scissors.

"I'm an Indian on the warpath and I'm scalping you!" he cried. *Snip! Snip!* A handful of Badger's brown hair dropped to the barn floor.

"Quit it!" yelled Badger, but he stopped punching at Fred. The sight of the great sharp scissors had taken all the fight out of him.

Snip Snip! Snip!

"There!" Fred said with satisfaction as he turned Badger loose. "That's the way the Indians do it."

Badger stood up, half bald-headed and crying. "I'll tell my father and he'll tell yours. You'll get a licking," he threatened.

Fred lost his sense of triumph. What would Father do! All of a sudden he didn't feel like an Indian on the warpath. He felt like a boy who sure as sure was going to get a licking.

It was a worried Fred who slipped into his chair at the big mahogany supper table that night. He could tell by their faces that his parents had already heard from Badger's father. Plump and pretty Mrs. Remington looked surprised that her son could be so naughty. Colonel Remington sat straight as though he were on a horse. He looked grave. The colonel had fought through four years of the Civil War, and commanded many men. He never wasted words. He wasted none now. He looked at Fred and asked, *"Why?"*

"I was making a sketchbook. Badger came in and threw it on the floor and tramped it in the dirt," Fred said.

"Before you cut his hair?" asked the colonel.

"Yes, sir."

Colonel Remington took a bite of food from his plate and ate it slowly before he said, "Then you both share the blame, and you have both been punished. You lost your sketchbook and he lost some hair. Clara, this is excellent chicken pie. Frederic, eat before your supper gets cold."

Fred knew that the subject of Badger was

closed. He should have been happy but he wasn't. He felt dreadful. *For Badger had been right.* They weren't eagle feathers, no matter what he called them. And he had been planning all along to draw an Indian warrior with chicken feathers in his hair!

"Fake things are no good," he told himself angrily as he climbed into bed that night. "What I need is a *real* eagle."

He heard his parents' voices coming from their room. His mother was saying. "Seth, why do you encourage the child in his foolish drawing?"

"It's a harmless pastime, my dear," his father replied. "Why shouldn't a boy who loves action and horses want to draw them? Have you looked at his sketches? Some of them are quite good. I think he may have a little talent."

"He must learn to make a living," Mrs. Remington said firmly.

"All in good time," answered the colonel. "Someday I hope he'll go into the newspaper office with me, but that is years in the future. In the meantime let the boy have his fun."

2. News from Far Places

Fred did have fun as the months sped by. His family was well known in Canton so there were many invitations to outings and parties, and many friends visited in the Remingtons' big two-story house.

His mother's parents, the Henry L. Sackriders, lived nearby in another big house that was a second home to the boy. He'd gotten his middle name from them: Frederic Sackrider Remington. His other grandfather, Samuel Remington, was a Universalist clergyman.

Often Fred visited the small stone fire station, Engine House No. 1, where he had been made

Members of Canton Engine House No. 1
with mascot, Fred Remington, center

the mascot because he "helped" put out fires. Colonel Remington's newspaper plant had burned twice. The first time, Fred helped pass buckets of water to the fire fighters from the little river at the foot of Main Street. The town had two bucket brigades—nicknamed the "Wooden and Tin Pail Companies."

By the time of the second fire, 1870, Canton boasted a small hand-pump machine with a hose attached to it. Fred thought it a magnificent piece of equipment. Proudly he marched beside it in the Fourth of July parade, wearing his fireman's visored cap, white gloves, and wide white belt.

In all Canton, though, the most interesting place to Fred was his own supper table. It was not because he liked to eat—although he did— but because he liked to hear his father tell the news that had come into the *Plaindealer* office during the day.

The news that fascinated the boy most were reports from the Far West, that vast land of plains and mountains stretching beyond the Mississippi River to the Pacific Ocean. It was a land still largely peopled by Indians, but more and more white settlers were moving onto Indian hunting grounds, and there were many clashes between white and red men.

Other exciting things were happening in the West, too, and easterners were eager to hear of them. Newspapers printed all the reports they could get about wagon trains and cattle drives, about the railroad pushing across the prairies, and about new gold strikes.

To Fred, even the names of those far-off places sounded exotic: Montana and Dakota Territories, the Staked Plains of Texas, the Oregon Trail, Santa Fe, the Rockies.

Most exciting of all, to his ears, was the news that his father told about war-painted Indians raiding frontier settlements. Sometimes they stole white children and carried them away, never to be seen again by their families.

Fred's eyes grew wide at these stories. What would it be like to be captured by Indians and live in a tepee and eat buffalo meat instead of ham and eggs?

Sometimes the United States Cavalry troopers rode after the Indians, the colonel said.

Then the boy's face grew dreamy. He could almost see the long line of blue-clad cavalrymen riding across the great bare plains. He could see their bright guidons—or flags—streaming in the breeze, and the dust rising from the horses' hoofs. He could hear the sharp sweet call of a bugle echoing across the empty land.

"I'm going West when I grow up," he said abruptly one night. "Maybe I'll be a soldier, or maybe I'll live in a tepee with the Indians."

"Why, Fred!" Mrs. Remington's voice sounded shocked. "The idea of living with savages who steal children! They are dreadful people!"

"Stealing children is not my idea of warfare," the colonel said mildly, "but the Indians do have their reasons, Clara. After all, we are driving them from their homes and land. It *is* their land, you know, although we seldom admit it publicly. We make treaties with them and break the treaties. Our hunters kill off the buffalo herds that have fed the Indians for generations.

"No wonder the red men fight back," the colonel went on. "As you say, their methods look dreadful to us—burning and scalping and stealing. But I suspect that a trooper with a gun looks just as dreadful to an Indian armed only with bow and arrows."

"Why are we driving them from their homes?" Fred asked.

The colonel smiled wryly. "Free land," he said. "We want all that free land and a chance for the nation to expand westward. You might call it a country's growing pains, Fred. Countries have them as well as children, and growing pains always hurt even though they're necessary."

"All the same, I won't have my only child going out there," Mrs. Remington said.

But he *would* go, the boy thought. As soon as he was old enough, he would travel all over the West, and he'd draw everything he saw. He'd fill more tablets with his sketches than a horse could carry. In the meantime, he must learn all he could about drawing. Already he'd found what a difference it made in a picture if you drew a line quickly

A Patrol.

An early sketch of Fred's, drawn on a schoolbook
page, showed his early interest in the cavalry.

or if you drew it slowly. Both lines were good,
but they said different things. He didn't understand why, he just knew it was true.

So each evening he sat in his room drawing
pictures of the thrilling events his father had
described at supper. His stubby fingers carefully
sketched Indians, or mounted troopers who
looked like his cavalryman father. It never oc-
curred to him to draw a house or flower or bird.

When Fred was eleven years old his father was
appointed to the post of Collector of the Port of

Ogdensburg, New York, on the St. Lawrence River. He sold his newspaper.

Ogdensburg was a bigger town than Canton, and Fred liked it, although he did not like attending school. Study bored him. He skipped classes when he could even though he knew his father would whip him for it. He preferred to roam the woods or sit under a tree sketching western scenes. Although he lived beside a great river, Fred never drew a picture of a boat. His father bought him good drawing paper and pencils now. He was sorry he couldn't please his father by liking school.

Fred was fifteen when his parents decided to send him to Highland Military Academy in Worcester, Massachusetts. The colonel believed that military training was the proper way to form character, and certainly so spirited and impulsive a boy as Fred needed good discipline.

Fred protested that he did not want to go all the way to Massachusetts to school. He felt bitter when his father ordered the textbooks he would need. It was all he could do to stand quietly when his mother measured him for the uniform the Academy tailor would make to fit Fred's big frame. He was 5′8″ tall now, and weighed 180 pounds.

"Just wait until your uniform comes," Mrs. Remington said patiently. "You'll like it, Fred."

When the textbooks arrived at Fred's home he began to feel better, for one was Upton's *Infantry Tactics*. Eagerly he pored over it. The drills looked good! The book didn't have the soldier illustrations he would have liked but that didn't matter. He'd draw his own.

Then his uniform came. It had three rows of brass buttons down the front and more on the sleeves. Fred put it on and stood before a mirror admiring his military appearance. He imagined himself marching on the parade grounds.

Snappily he saluted himself in the mirror. He threw back his shoulders and took a few marching steps. Excitement began to rise in him. Why, it would be great to wear a uniform and drill!

For the first time in his life, Fred Remington wanted to go to school.

3. Art and Football

One of Fred's good friends at Highland was Julian Wilder. The two boys, who belonged to the same military squad, played pranks together and shared a love for sports. It didn't spoil their friendship at all when, in a wrestling match, Fred gave Julian a broken shoulder blade, a broken collar bone, and a dislocated arm! Big strapping Fred had not realized his own strength.

One day Julian received a letter from Scott Turner, a boy back in Julian's hometown of Augusta, Maine. Scott had studied art, and he'd decorated his letter with pen-and-ink sketches of soldiers on horseback.

Julian showed Fred some of the drawings.

"They're grand!" exclaimed the delighted Fred. "Give me his address. I'm going to write to him tonight!"

That surprised Julian who had always thought Fred was a bit bashful. But Fred Remington was never bashful when the subject was art.

Soon Fred was at his desk composing a letter.

"March 3, 1877. Dear Scott," he began. "You draw splendidly. I admire your mode of shading which I cannot get the 'hang' of. Your favorite subject is soldiers. So is mine."

Scott answered Fred's letter and soon the young artists were sending one another samples of their work. Fred had never had an art lesson so he learned much from Scott, but he did not like it when Scott sent him drawings of men and women in fancy clothes. "Don't send me any more women or any more dudes," he wrote Scott. "Send me Indians, cowboys, villains, or toughs. These are what I want. Give me a battle between Russians and Turks, or Indians and soldiers." By now Fred was working with paint and paintbrush as well

Fred Remington in the uniform of the Highland Military Academy in Worcester, Massachusetts

as with drawing pencil. The use of colors made art more exciting than ever to him.

One day Scott wrote asking for a photograph of Fred.

Fred sent it, but he sent a letter with it that said:

"I don't see what you want with such a looking thing as this. You can burn it up but don't throw it into the back yard or it may scare some wandering hen to death." Actually Fred was a handsome youth, even if he didn't know it. He told Scott, "I don't amount to anything in particular. I can spoil an immense amount of good grub at any time in the day. I go a good man on muscle. My hair is short and stiff. There is nothing poetical about me."

Fred still shied away from books, but nobody was more energetic at carrying a musket on the parade ground. His good humor made everyone like him, even his instructors who couldn't get him to study. However, he did do well in his English class for which he wrote excellent themes.

After two years Fred left Highland. Military

school hadn't changed him as his father had hoped it would. Still, one thing had been accomplished. By now Fred's mother realized that her son had no interest in business, only in art. She agreed that Fred could go to Yale's new School of Art.

Fred was almost seventeen when he arrived at Yale College in New Haven, Connecticut. At last he was really going to learn how to draw and paint! Eagerly he went to his first class.

The class was held in a dark and gloomy basement room, and there were only two students— Fred and a youth named Poultney Bigelow, who was nicknamed "Big." The boys stared around them in disappointment. The dingy place was chiefly furnished with plaster copies of ancient Greek statues. Fred disliked them on sight.

The art professor was a pleasant man but when he explained the first lesson assignment, Fred's heart sank.

The assignment was for Fred and Big to draw a picture of one of the statues—a plaster copy of "The Faun" which had been carved in marble by a Greek sculptor in the fourth century B.C.

The faun was a young man, almost nude, leaning idly against a tree trunk as he looked off into the distance. He held a flute in one hand, and he had a panther skin slung carelessly across his body. It didn't look like a panther skin to Fred. It didn't look like much of anything.

"The sculptor was Praxiteles, who lived in Athens," said the professor. "He came from a family of artists and he was famous for filling his statues with the emotions of the soul."

He pointed to "The Faun." "Look at this statue," he said. "It is only a poor copy of the marble youth Praxiteles created. But even in this copy you can see that the sculptor was expressing a feeling of sweet dreaming in a musical mood."

Fred Remington looked hard at "The Faun." He could see that Praxiteles had been a great sculptor, but Fred didn't want to learn to draw statues of sweet dreaming. He wanted to draw battle scenes, and stampeding cattle, and cowboys roping wild horses.

With a sigh he picked up his pencil. "I guess we have to do it," he said to Big.

Fred was a member of the Yale football squad,
above. He is seated at the far right.

That was the first of many lessons about
European art antiquities, and Fred found them
all dull.

Disappointed in his art class, Fred decided to
go out for sports. He became Yale's heavyweight
boxing champion. He made the varsity football
team. College football was a rough game then,
which was exactly the sort of game Fred liked.
He played end and soon became outstanding. It
was through football that he first had one of his
drawings published.

Poultney Bigelow was editor of the *Yale Courant*, an illustrated college magazine put out by the students. Big and Fred had become good friends, and Big asked Fred to draw something for the magazine. Fred drew a humorous cartoon of a student football player wrapped in bandages who—it was plain to see—had just fought a hard game and suffered a lot of damage.

Proudly Fred sent his parents a copy of the magazine which published his drawing. Just looking at that picture made him feel like a real artist!

4. The Trail West

Sorrow came to Fred during his second year at Yale. Colonel Remington died.

The loss of his father hit Fred hard, for the colonel had been his hero. Fred loved horses because his father had taught him to love them. He first drew soldiers because his father had been a cavalryman. English was Fred's best school subject and he liked to write because his father had been a writer and newspaperman.

"I'm not going back to Yale," Fred told his mother one night after the funeral as the two sat alone in the big Ogdensburg house. "All I do there is box and play football. With Father gone, I should be earning money. I'm going to get a job."

"But your art!" exclaimed Mrs. Remington. "Your father left you some money, so you don't need to go to work immediately. Don't you want to continue studying art?"

"Not the classroom kind," Fred told her. "I'm not interested in studying European art and copying old masters."

He didn't know how to explain it to his mother, or even to himself, but in all his studies he had found only a few European artists whom he admired.

The chief one was Edouard Detaille, a French painter of history and military scenes. Detaille's horseback soldiers were done in such exact detail that Fred thought they looked real enough to gallop right out of the picture. To paint like Detaille—that would be something! Yet Fred knew that he was not any nearer to it now than he was on that first day at Yale when he and Big drew "The Faun."

"What kind of job will you get?" Mrs. Remington asked.

"Some kind of office work—you always said

you wanted me to settle down and be a business-man, Mother. And I can still draw and paint at night. Leaving school won't mean I'm leaving art."

Fred found a job clerking in the office of the governor of New York State, but after a few weeks he grew bored, put on his coat, and walked out. He was too restless to spend his days at a desk, adding long columns of figures. The four walls of an office seemed like a prison to him. He took various office jobs trying to find one he liked, but quit them all. People began to say that Fred Remington would never amount to much.

That summer of 1880 Fred went back to Canton to visit. Friends took him to the county fair to see the horses, and there he met Eva Adele Caten.

Eva's home was in Gloversville, New York, but she too was visiting in Canton. When Fred looked at her he saw a pretty girl in a lacy dress of blue that matched her blue eyes. She had a sweet smile and a bubbling personality. When Eva looked at Fred she saw a blondish young man who was handsome, heavyset, not tall but powerfully built.

While a brass band played rollicking music, and the holiday crowd laughed and chattered and ate fresh peach ice cream, Eva and Fred fell in love.

On Eva's return to Gloversville Fred followed her and, as was the custom then, asked her father for her hand.

"How do you plan to support my daughter?" inquired Mr. Lawton Caten. He was a practical, successful businessman who had five children and knew what it cost to raise a family.

The embarrassed Fred mumbled something about being an artist.

Mr. Caten shook his gray head. "Art is a risky business, and you're not prepared for anything else. You didn't finish college. You didn't even keep a simple clerk's job. No, Fred, you aren't ready to marry. I'm sorry, but I have to think of Eva's future."

It was a bitter and disappointed youth who returned to Ogdensburg, his hopes smashed. And it was a hard blow to his pride to realize that people had been right. He didn't amount to anything!

He wasn't cut out for a businessman, yet he'd never earned a penny with his art. What else could he do to make money? He'd won the heavy-weight boxing championship at Yale—should he become a professional boxer? Did boxers make enough money to support a pretty and fashionable wife?

"What I need is a gold mine!" he thought rue-fully.

Then he knew what he could do. There had been much talk of a new gold strike in Montana. Why not go there and make a quick fortune min-ing gold? That should prove that he could support Eva!

Mrs. Remington was reluctant to see her only child go so far away, but she knew that Fred had been deeply hurt and was in a reckless mood. Per-haps a change of scene would do him good. She agreed he should use some of his small inheritance from his father and make the trip.

On a crisp October morning shortly after his nineteenth birthday, Fred Remington began the long journey by train, steamboat, and stagecoach to Montana. He had always wanted to go to that land of cowboys and Indians, but he had wanted to go for the thrill of adventure, not just to get rich. He had wanted to sketch what he saw, but now he hadn't even packed a drawing pencil in his luggage.

Although this was not the way he'd dreamed his trip would start, he still felt a stir of excitement. It would be fine to come back a wealthy man! For the first time since his talk with Mr. Caten, Fred began to feel good again. Smiling, he stared from the window as the little train picked up speed and the wheels clacked on the iron rails that led west.

5. Big Land, Big Sky

Montana Territory in 1880 was a wild and rough land. To the youth fresh from New York State it seemed too raw and rugged to believe, and he was not surprised when people told him that Montana was the most isolated territory in the West. Often his fingers itched for a pencil to draw the vast prairies and granite mountains, and the boisterous, hard-living men. He shrugged the feeling aside, reminding himself that he was here to make a fortune.

He bought a saddle horse and rode to several frontier towns to get acquainted with the region.

They were "shack towns" by eastern standards

—one-room houses and stores built of raw lumber along streets ankle-deep with dust or mud. There were few women, but every town was jammed with weather-toughened men who moved briskly down the board sidewalks, spurs jingling.

Fascinated, Fred stood on the streets of Helena and watched the freight outfits—big canvas-covered wagons pulled by mules or oxen. They transported supplies from the East to the West's frontier towns and military posts—food, clothing, tools, everything from mirrors to mail. Sometimes as many as three wagons were hitched together and drawn by teams of twelve mules. Burly drivers swung sixteen-foot whips above the heads of the animals. The snap of the lashes sounded sharp as rifle shots.

There were saloons, dance halls, cafes, livery stables. There were cowboys in from the open range—mule skinners—bullwhackers shouting at oxen yoked to high-wheeled wagons. Quiet Indians, wearing deerskin leggings and blanket robes, strolled down the main street. On one corner a traveling minister preached to a small crowd, and on another a loud-voiced gambler cried his game.

Fred could have watched forever, but he was anxious to get to the mines. One noon he was in a little cafe. Over a plate of beans at a long wooden table, he asked his tablemates where to find gold.

The old-timers looked with amusement at the pink-cheeked youth in his stylishly-cut eastern clothes.

"Planning on staying with us for a while, are you, sonny?" asked one graybeard with a smile.

This Remington drawing of cowboys coming to town at Christmas was typical of westerners Fred met.

"I'm just going to stay long enough to make a million dollars," Fred said innocently.

The men roared with laughter. They reared back in their chairs and slapped their knees and laughed so hard that they nearly choked on their beans. Then they saw the young man's face redden with embarrassment, and they grew quiet. "Ever done any placer digging?" one asked kindly.

Fred shook his head. "What is it?"

They looked as if they wanted to laugh again at this ignorant kid with the million-dollar ideas. Instead they explained that placer digging was breaking your back with a pick and shovel digging up sand and gravel that might—just might—contain particles of gold. You washed the sand and gravel to find out. You could dig and wash for a long time and not find enough gold to pay for the grub you were eating.

"I might be lucky," Fred said. "Anyway, I'm going to try. How do I get to the goldfield?"

"You don't get there this time of year," the graybeard said. "The diggings are in the gulches and high mountains over west—in the northern

Rockies. A hard place to get to anytime, and a hard place to live in all the time. Nobody tries either one in winter. Fellows are leaving there now and won't go back till spring. Wait till spring to break your back, sonny. That's soon enough not to find your million dollars."

The other men nodded agreement. "Never was as much placer gold in Montana as people think," one said. "We've got deep-down gold, and silver and copper, too, but it'll take real mining operations to get them. That means time, and money for machinery. A lone man can't do it with a shovel. I'll make my million"—he grinned at Fred —"running beef cattle. That's easier than panning gold and a lot surer."

Out on the street again, Fred shivered in the sharp wind. Spring seemed a long time off. Meanwhile he guessed he'd ride around and look the country over.

He began to live in the saddle, riding where his fancy took him. It was a big land under a big sky and from childhood he'd dreamed of seeing it. Now he prowled the trails.

Early darkness overtook him one cold evening between towns. When he spied a campfire he stopped. Beside it a grizzled freighter sat eating bacon out of a frying pan. A smoke-blackened coffeepot bubbled over the wood coals.

"Howdy, young feller. Come and rest yourself," the old man said with the hospitality that Fred had learned to expect in the West. The man's cotton shirt was open at the neck as though he did not feel the cold. In the gathering dusk Fred could see a shabby wagon standing under a bare-branched tree, and horses staked nearby.

Soon Fred was sharing the bacon and warming his fingers around a tin cup of hot black coffee.

"Where you from?" the freighter asked.

"New York State."

"Me, too. But I had a hankering to see the West when I was about your age, so I moved west to Iowa. When it got crowded there, I came to Montana. Now its getting crowded here. Too many people have come in." He looked at Fred and chuckled. "Like you and me.

"And now," he continued, "there is no more

West. In a few years the railroad will come along the Yellowstone and a poor man won't be able to make an honest living at all."

For the rest of his life Fred Remington would remember that night and tell about it.

"I saw men already swarming into the land in a restless surge," Fred said. Soon, he realized, there would be fences and plowed fields—and railroad cars instead of freight wagons like his friend's. There would be big cities, and the smoking chimneys of great factories would pierce Montana skies.

"I knew the wild riders and the vacant land were about to vanish forever," Fred said later, "and the more I considered the subject the bigger the forever loomed."

Snow began to fall on the old man and the boy sitting beside the campfire. Fred scarcely noticed. A strange sort of excitement had gripped him. At last he saw a purpose for his life! Perhaps he would never earn big money, but money didn't matter when something important needed doing that he could do.

He wasn't sure exactly how to begin, but he was going to draw and paint frontier America before it disappeared forever. He would put everything about it down on paper and canvas, and he'd put it down truly and honestly so that men who knew would look at his pictures and say, "Yes, that's the way the West was." He'd begin tomorrow.

The old freighter threw more wood on the fire. "Time to turn in," he said.

They rolled up in their saddle blankets. Soon they were asleep, while the snow fell softly and somewhere far off a wolf pointed his sharp nose to the sky and howled his hunger.

6. In the Saddle

For the next two years Frederic Remington wandered over the West. He rode from Montana and the Dakotas south through Wyoming, Colorado, and Kansas to the far Southwest and even into old Mexico. He became an artist on horseback, and his studio was in his saddlebags.

Since he had no proper drawing materials, he used rough wrapping paper that he picked up in frontier stores, and cheap tablets that reminded him of the two-penny tablets he used to buy back in Canton.

At first his sketches were crude. He had been drawing since childhood, but his previous drawings were imaginary scenes of western life.

"*Ceremony of the Scalps*"

"An Old Time Plains Fight"

"*The Emigrants*"

51

"Downing the Nigh Leader"

52

Now Fred faced the real thing, and he soon learned that he had to train his eye as well as his hand. He had to learn to see a scene in all its detail as well as to draw it.

A lesser artist might have been satisfied to skip some details, or draw them carelessly. Fred was determined to make his work realistic portrayals of the West. Every detail must be as accurate as if it were part of a history book. Moreover, he wanted every picture to tell a story. He thought the action should show the story so clearly that the picture would hardly need a title.

As he worked he recalled bits of lessons he had learned in his Yale art class. He remembered especially a lesson about the value of lines in a drawing. A vertical line gave a drawing strength. "Think of a cathedral," the professor had said. Instead, Fred thought now of a ponderosa pine, the tree that grew so tall and straight in Montana.

A horizontal line suggested repose and rest, like a prairie or still water. Curved lines imparted beauty; a blade of grass was curved. Slanting lines gave a feeling of action, while conflicting lines

Fred learned how to be a cowboy. This photograph
shows cowhands of the 1880s branding steers.

suggested great action or turmoil—a battle or a
herd of stampeding cattle. He was seeing plenty
of slanting and conflicting lines, Fred thought as
he ranged the West and made himself a part of it.

He hired out as a cowboy on cattle ranches in
Montana and later in Texas; his young strength
and good horsemanship made it easy for him to
find jobs. On the ranches he learned to throw a
lariat over the head of the wildest steer, just as he

had dreamed of doing as a boy. He learned first-hand the hot dusty work of branding, and the lonely quiet of riding "night herd" when cowboys sang to calm the restless cattle.

He learned the dangers of a stampede. Those dangers were among the realities of ranch life that he said "burned into my brain." Of cattle stampeded at night by lightning, he said:

> I think the animal man was never called on to do a more desperate deed than running in the night with long-horns taking the country as it came and with the cattle splitting out behind him, all as mad as the thunder and lightning above him, while the cut banks and prairie dog holes wait below. Nature is merciless.

In later years Fred painted many superb pictures of ranch life—scenes from his own days as a cowboy. Sometimes he even painted or drew himself into the pictures. One of the earliest of his

Fred remembered his life among the cowboys when
he later drew "In from the Night Herd."

cowboy pictures is called "In from the Night Herd" and shows a weary young puncher returning to camp after long hours of work. The puncher is thought to be a likeness of the artist himself.

Besides working on ranches, Fred spent much time with various Indian tribes. Most of the Indians lived on government reservations, and there were still many whites who were afraid of them and would not go among them.

Fred felt no such fear. He admired the red men as brave hunters, and soldiers, and as fine horsemen. He made friends with many of them.

Among the splendid Indian pictures he painted later are portraits of individuals: "A Reservation Comanche," "A Cheyenne Agency Policeman," "A Kiowa Buck," "A Yuma Apache," "A Crow Scout." He also painted scenes of Indian buffalo hunts, ceremonial dances, and tribal life.

Most exciting of all to Fred in those years of roaming were the periods he spent with parties of United States Cavalry who patrolled the plains and maintained order.

Although he was not a trooper, Fred rode with

the cavalrymen and shared their lives. Out of his experiences with the army of the West came more great pictures: "Boots and Saddles," "Night Halt of Cavalry," "The Charge," "The Pursuit," and many more.

However, these paintings were all in the future. During the two years Fred wandered over the West, from the northern plains of Montana to the hot sands of Arizona and old Mexico, he did not know that he was storing memories. He only knew there was so much to see and learn that no day was long enough for him.

Wherever he went, in frontier towns or on the dim trails of the back country, his hands were busy putting into sketches all that he saw. They were practice sketches, for he was learning technique with each one. Perhaps it was a buffalo attacking a crippled steer, or Indian boys running a race. Perhaps there were hungry cowhands waiting impatiently by the ranch chuck wagon for the cook's call of "Come and get it!" Onto the sketch pads they went—scene after scene—until the stack of drawings began to make Fred's saddlebags bulge.

Fred sketched the "types" of cowboys who peopled the West and "cowboy fun." His sketches became the basis for his most successful drawings.

He was in Arizona when he drew his first published sketch. The pay was ten dollars and the sketch was called "Cowboys of Arizona." It showed cowhands being awakened from their sleep by a scout who brought word that danger was near. Fred drew it on wrapping paper, folded it, put it into an envelope, and mailed it to an eastern magazine. *Harper's Weekly* published the picture in February, 1882.

When his mother sent him a copy of the magazine, Fred was disappointed to see that under his picture was the credit-line: "Drawn by W.A. Rogers from a sketch by Frederic Remington."

Fred knew only too well what that meant. His sketch hadn't been good enough. Another man had to redo it.

Long years later Fred Remington met W.A. Rogers. Rogers told Fred how the picture had arrived in its crumpled envelope, and, although it lacked the polish of professional work, it had impressed the *Harper's* editors as worth publishing. So it had been given to Rogers, who was a staff man on the magazine, to redraw. Rogers told

Fred he remembered with how much pleasure he had worked with Fred's sketch. "I recall having admired it greatly," he said.

"You introduced me to the public," Fred replied. "I was mighty glad I fell into the hands of an artist who knew a cowboy saddle and a western horse."

However, all that was in the future. When Fred first saw that his picture had been redrawn, he only knew that he'd have to work harder. Vigorously he set about it, and the saddlebags bulged with more and more sketches.

After two years of roaming, Fred decided it was time to go back home to see his mother and Eva Caten. He hadn't made any money. He still couldn't marry Eva, but he could tell her that he was becoming a better artist and had a job he'd stay with the rest of his life.

7. A Ranch in Kansas

"Go on, Terra Cotta!" Fred shouted as he tapped the big mare lightly with his spur. "There's a jack! Let's get him!"

Over the Kansas plains they raced after the jack rabbit—the gold-colored horse with yellow mane and tail flying, and Fred Remington in the saddle brandishing a small wooden pole. It was great fun "coursing" rabbits, which meant getting close enough to a jack to touch him with one's pole. Fred threw himself into the sport with his usual wholehearted vigor.

The wise jack had played this game before. It dodged into some brush, then doubled back on its trail. In a moment its long ears were lost from sight in the tall prairie grass.

"Never mind, girl." Fred patted the mare. "We had a good run, and so did the jack. We'll all feel better for the exercise."

He turned the horse toward home.

"Home" to Fred now was a sheep ranch near the little town of Peabody, Kansas, which was close to Kansas City. It had been six months since Fred had made the trip back East to see his mother and Eva. While there he'd heard from Robert Camp, an old Yale friend. Bob was raising sheep in Kansas and making good money. He persuaded Fred to buy a ranch next to his.

So in the spring of 1883, when he was twenty-one years old, Fred spent the last of his inheritance to become a sheep rancher. Once again he had hope of a steady income. Eva was still waiting for him.

The ranch was a nice place—320 acres of blue stem grass. Fred had a three-room frame house, well, corral, shed, and barn. He had several hundred sheep, his fine horse Terra Cotta, and many friends. His friends were young ranchers, like Bob Camp, who lived nearby. They were gay, fun-loving men who liked to gather at Fred's place to talk, smoke, drink, eat, and box. Boxing was a favorite sport with them, but few wanted to box with Fred.

"Come on, Bob," Fred sometimes begged, "put on the gloves with me."

"No, sir!" Bob laughed. "I haven't forgotten you were Yale champ. Anyway, you're too big for me." Fred was indeed growing bigger. Despite his active life, he continued to gain weight.

Another friend was a cheery, red-faced English-man whom everybody called "Charlie B." Charlie B. owned a horse ranch seven miles away. Often he started out late in the evening to visit Fred, and rode over the lonely prairie, arriving at his friend's about two A.M. When Fred climbed from his blanket and sleepily answered the door, Charlie B. bounced in with a hearty "Hello, Fred. Hello, my boy," and sat down for a nice long chat with his friend.

"Say, what's the matter with the daytime for

calling on a fellow?" poor Fred protested, but sociable Charlie B. never took the hint.

While a hired hand tended the sheep, Fred sketched and painted. Fred was also the ranch cook, but he would have won no cooking prizes. His chief "dishes" were sardines and canned tomatoes.

Fred needed the ranch not only for income but as a permanent place to work. His collection of drawings had grown too large to carry around on horseback. Morever, he wanted to try oil painting and that required space for supplies. He didn't really like the sheep. He had no taste for the work of dipping, lambing, and wool shearing. Although he made sketches of his flock, he had more fun carving a picture of a cowboy on the barn wall.

He sketched his ranch, his neighbors' ranches, Terra Cotta. He went to the Plum Grove schoolhouse and sketched the minister who came there to preach each Sunday. For Bob Camp's cook he sketched a picture of a cow defending her calf from wolves.

Although he was now a rancher, Fred kept on

"And may the best man win".

Any thing for a quiet life.

Remington drew these sketches describing life on his Kansas sheep ranch.

the move, making notes and drawings for future work. One trip took him to Dodge City, then the cowboy capital of the world. Another time he rode Terra Cotta into Indian Territory, now Oklahoma, where the Comanches lived. A third trip took them through deep coulees and over broad mesas, dodging prairie dog holes and tumbleweed, all the way to Apache country in New Mexico.

On these sketching trips Fred slept on the ground with his saddle for a pillow. He said he had a thick mattress and a big counterpane, meaning he had the earth as a mattress and the whole sky for a cover. Mornings, he was up while the stars were still shining in a black sky. He ate bacon and drank coffee at his campfire while the sun came up and chased the night's gray shadows over the western hills.

Those magnificent sunrises delighted his artist's eye for color. As he watched the sun shine against a rocky bluff, he could see a painter's whole palette in the scene.

When he returned to his ranch house from a trip, he set up his easel in the long living room.

Then he tried to recapture the scenes and colors he had stored in his memory. He experimented with mixing paints, with "composition" which is the placing of figures on a canvas, with light and shadow, and all the other problems that face a painter.

Spring came again, and with it the season for clipping and selling wool. However, in that spring of 1884 the price of wool dropped disastrously, and Fred made no money. Sheep had been a poor investment, he realized. He sold the ranch and moved to a little house on the outskirts of Kansas City.

Now he began painting in earnest, and even sold a few paintings. William W. Findlay, a Kansas City storekeeper, hung some of Fred's oils in his store and sold what he could.

Fred began to write stories, too. He wrote and illustrated one about the sheep ranch, Terra Cotta, and the jacks. He called it "Coursing Rabbits on the Plains." Almost three years later, in May 1887, *Outing Magazine* published the tale, and Fred Remington's career as a writer began.

In Kansas, Fred drew this self-portrait entitled "Boss of the 'Badger State' in Spring Lambing."

Sometimes Fred found it hard to work. In Kansas City, as in Peabody, he had too many noisy friends who dropped in to visit. Fred was a jovial host, and generous with food and drink.

He was very active physically and missed the wide-open spaces of the sheep ranch. Sometimes in summer dawns he picked up his lariat, got on his horse, and rode out into the country. Then across the prairies he raced and whooped, and lassoed sunflowers as though they were longhorn steers.

One day he realized that his money from the sale of the ranch was disappearing fast. He'd spent a lot on entertaining his friends, and also in buying cowboy and Indian articles for the studio he hoped someday to have. He'd bought eagle feather headdresses, old guns, fine saddles, branding irons, beaded war shirts—everything that represented the frontier West. All had been sent to his mother for safekeeping.

Perhaps it would be wise to invest the money he had left in a business, he told himself. He bought a one-third interest in a Kansas City saloon. Prospects were bright for a good income. He and Eva set their wedding date for early fall.

Then suddenly Fred was cheated of every penny. It was a terrible blow to him, but he decided to say nothing of his loss. Instead, he would try to earn the money back by working harder at his art.

In the Caten home in Gloversville, he and Eva were married on October 1, 1884. It was Fred's twenty-third birthday. Now he was a proud young husband with a lovely and loyal wife.

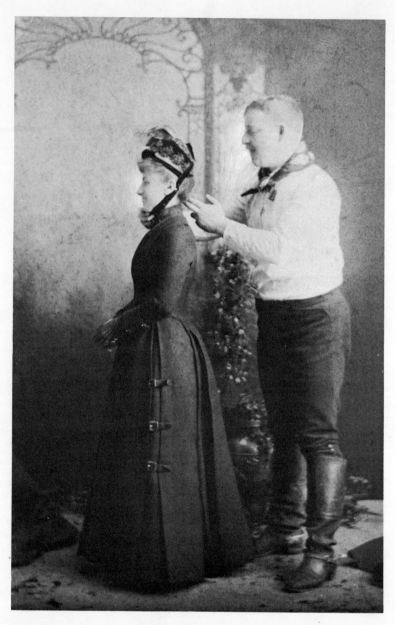

An early photograph of Fred and Eva Remington

8. Apache Land

Fred and Eva—he called her "Missie"—set up housekeeping in Fred's house in Kansas City. They were happy but poor.

Up at six o'clock every morning, Fred sketched and painted all day. He submitted many sketches to eastern magazines but sold only one. It was called "Ejecting an Oklahoma Boomer" and showed soldiers ousting a white squatter who had illegally settled on Indian reservation land. *Harper's Weekly* published the picture in March, 1885, but again there was a disappointing credit line: "Drawn by T. de Thulstrup from a sketch by Frederic Remington." A gloomy Fred took no pleasure in it.

The young couple sold personal possessions—even Fred's horse—for money to live on. By spring they were desperate. Fred's mother came west to visit. She was indignant when she saw their plight.

"Give up this foolish idea of being an artist," she told Fred. "Come home with me and go into a respectable business."

Fred shook his head. He and Eva had already made a decision. She would go back to her family and wait while he tried to get a new start farther west. They hoped they would not be parted very long.

After Eva left, Fred sold the rest of their house furnishings. Now almost everything he owned was in his pocket. He stood on a street corner undecided what to do next. "Shorty" Reason, a house painter, drove by in a wagon pulled by a stout gray horse. Fred liked its looks and he was a good judge of horseflesh.

"Want to sell that mare?" he called to Shorty.

"Nope." Shorty stopped anyway, to show that he might if the price were right.

"Is she good under the saddle?" Fred asked.

Shorty shrugged. "Try her for yourself." He began to unhitch the big mare. Since Fred now weighed 200 pounds he needed a big horse.

Fred borrowed a saddle and soon he was astride the gray. She was strong and easily handled. He paid Shorty fifty dollars for her.

At sunrise next day Fred headed southwest. There was talk of a gold discovery in the Pinal Range of Arizona Territory and he meant to go there. This time, he promised himself, no gray-beard would talk him out of trying to find a stake.

Fred joined two other prospectors, and together they dug and sweated in the desert mountains.

The summer sun was like a furnace overhead. The sands were scorching hot. Danger lurked nearby, for the Apache Indians—under their fierce chief Geronimo—were waging war on white men.

The Apaches were the most dangerous Indians in all the West. Their hatred for whites who had usurped their land was deep and savage, and they weren't afraid of cavalry troopers. Fred quickly realized he'd picked a poor time to come to the Pinal Range.

One night after supper he and his companions lay under a tree beside their cooking fire, talking idly. Half asleep, Fred stared up at a far-off star that twinkled between the tree's black branches. Suddenly something made him sit up. He gasped in astonishment.

On the other side of the fire, silent as ghosts, sat three Apaches. Their rifles lay across their laps, and they were watching Fred with hard, unblinking eyes.

"Heap hungry," one said.

The other prospectors jerked up. They too gasped. One made a move to reach for his gun.

"We White Mountain people. No want fight—want flour," the Apache said.

Cautiously Fred got up and made a pack of flour and some bacon. One of the prospectors pushed the remains of the supper to the Indians' side of the fire.

The visitors ate unhurriedly, while the gold hunters watched the firelight glint on their swarthy, high-cheekboned faces and coarse black hair, so long it brushed their shoulders.

When they had finished eating, the Indians stretched out on the ground and went to sleep.

Fred and his friends lay back and pretended to sleep, too, but Fred did not close his eyes all night. He did not trust the uninvited guests. How had they come so quietly—making no more noise than a wisp of smoke? How many more Apaches were hidden behind the rocks and dark trees just outside the campfire's glow? At any moment he expected a screaming horde to spring out at him. It would not have surprised him to see an Apache drop from the tree branch above his head.

In the morning the Indians left. They took with them not only the flour and bacon but the gold hunters' sense of safety. The prospectors knew now that a phantom enemy might attack them at any moment, and with no more warning than a shadow gives.

"Let's get out of here," one said. "This is a bad place for white men, and there's no gold anyway."

They broke camp. Fred and his gray mare wandered the trails again. When he met a cavalry command, Fred rode with the troopers to the San

Remington took his easel with him and sketched the colorful life of the West as he wandered.

Carlos Reservation on Arizona's Gila River. It was home to those Apaches who had surrendered.

For a long time Fred had wanted to sketch Apaches, but the half-wild warriors of the desert would never stand still for him. Even the friendliest were suspicious of the white man's bits of paper and strange writing stick. The moment Fred took his eyes from an Apache he was sketching, the Apache simply melted away.

This time Fred was lucky. It was ration day at San Carlos and the Indians had come in from miles around to get their share of the freshly-slaughtered beef.

They came on mules, horses, burros, and they made a colorful scene as they thronged around the low adobe buildings of the agency. It was the sort of scene to delight an artist's heart. Fred sketched rapidly, and for once the Indians were too busy to notice.

He sketched girls wearing strange bright ornaments in their hair, bronzed young braves astride their ponies, women clutching great sides of beef, half-naked children romping in the sunshine, a fat and dignified chief. When ration day ended, Fred's saddlebags were growing heavy again with drawings.

Once more he took to the road. On Texas' grassy plains he met a cowboy, called Tex, who was also riding north. Together they jogged into western Oklahoma, which was Comanche country.

Fred liked the Comanches because they handled horses well and were the best riders he'd seen.

Their spotted pinto—or "painted"—ponies fascinated him.

"The best place to study horses is in an Indian camp," Fred told Tex. "Indians let their horses develop naturally. The ponies eat grass in summer, and the bark of cottonwood trees in winter, and thrive on both."

Fred never lost his love for horses. In his wanderings he constantly studied and sketched them. In later years he wrote many articles about them.

"Indian Reservation Horse Race"

He told about the Spanish horses of old Mexico, about the cayuse of Montana, and the far-western mustang. He described the characteristics of Texas piebalds, United States Cavalry mounts, and the little Cherokee ponies with their abundant manes and tails.

The cowboy broncos and Indian ponies were seldom beautiful, he admitted, but they had strength and power, and were intelligent. As saddle horses, they had no superior, he said.

"The best test of a horse is not what he can do but how easily he can do it," Fred Remington wrote in an article later, adding that the western horse could do everything easily.

Summer was at an end. The leaves of the cottonwoods turned yellow and prairie grass dried to a dull stubble. Tex said it was time for him to head back to Texas. Fred told his friend good-bye and turned the gray mare's nose toward Kansas City.

9. Pictures for Sale

In lavender twilight Fred rode into a little town across the Kansas border. He left his horse in a livery stable and went into the one small hotel. He was tired and hungry, and he was homesick for Eva, but he had no money to travel to New York.

As he passed through the barroom a familiar sight caught his eye. Two professional gamblers were "plucking a pigeon." The pigeon—an eastern salesman unwise in the ways of the West—was playing poker with the gamblers and being cheated with every deal of the cards.

Fred had seen much the same scene in many frontier towns. He didn't know these gamblers, but he knew their kind. They were masters of the stacked deck and the hidden card. They pretended to be strangers to one another, but they were really partners. A pigeon didn't have a chance against them.

Fred paused at the table to watch.

"I've got three kings," the salesman announced.

"That beats me," said one gambler, pretending disappointment.

"But not me," said his confederate. "I've got three aces." He showed them and raked in the pot. There was quite a lot of money in it.

The first gambler smiled at the pigeon. "Our luck's bound to change," he said smoothly.

Fred felt himself grow angry. The easterner was a poor fellow out trying to make a living, but these crooks wouldn't leave him a nickel. He tapped the salesman's shoulder. "Friend," he said, "take the advice of a well-wisher and go to bed. Your luck won't change."

His voice told more than his words, and suddenly the easterner understood. He arose from his chair. "Thieves!" he said scornfully.

With an oath one gambler reached under his coat as though to draw a gun. Fred whipped out his own gun and covered his friend's retreat.

In the salesman's bedroom they locked the door, and Fred stayed the night—with the oil lamp turned low and his gun ready. Once they heard stealthy steps on the creaking boards of the hall floor and saw the doorknob move. The gamblers were still after the pigeon's money.

"I've got a gun pointed straight at that door," shouted Fred. The stealthy steps moved on down the hall.

"What can I do to repay you?" the salesman asked Fred the next morning.

"I want to go to New York and haven't the price of a ticket," Fred said. "If you can afford it, you can pay my fare." The grateful easterner could afford it.

After selling his horse and paying his bills, Fred arrived in New York City with three dollars in his pocket. Under his arm he carried a portfolio bursting with sketches. It had been almost five years since he first came west as a youth of nineteen.

Eva joined him and they went to live with friends while Fred tried to sell his pictures.

He had no success. Although he had not realized it, his subject matter was unpopular then. Magazine editors did not want sketches of a wild, untamed West. It was to the national interest to persuade easterners to settle the vast region beyond the Mississippi, and so it must be pictured as a land of fertile farms and prosperous people. Who would migrate to a West where life was hard and dangerous?

Fred might have given up but Eva would not let him. His uncle, William Remington, loaned him some money so that he could attend classes at the Art Students League.

As an artist, Fred was self-taught. His only art lessons had been at Yale and he had skipped many of the classes. Now he worked hard in the league classes for he knew he needed technical instruction. Still he did not want to copy the work of others. He wanted to draw and paint in his own way, and he thought the subject matter of a picture more important than the technique. He had no desire to paint "beautiful" pictures, either. He thought being true to fact was of more value than decorative beauty.

So Fred Remington's real school was the school of experience and his best classroom was the West itself.

Fred continued to walk the streets of the great city peddling his pictures. He had no money for streetcars or hansom cabs, nor for new clothes. In his rough western garb he looked like a cowboy just off the ranch.

One day he hit luck in the office of *Harper's Weekly*, the only magazine that had used any of his work. He met J. Henry Harper, the publisher.

Mr. Harper looked at Fred's sketches. "They have the ring of new and live material," he said.

Apparently he did not care that Fred's West was not "pretty," for he bought a sketch. It was called "The Apache War: Indian Scouts on Geronimo's Trail." It appeared on the magazine's front cover of January 9, 1886. Best of all, it was not redrawn and so it carried Fred's name alone.

Fred sold two more sketches as illustrations for

This drawing of Fred's appeared on the cover of
Harper's Weekly in January 1886. He was elated that
it carried his name alone.

children's stories and two for a book about Mexico, but these few sales were little to show for five years' hard work.

It was a discouraged young artist who climbed the stairs to the attic office of the popular *Outing Magazine* one wintry day.

The art editor sat at his cluttered desk, hard at work on some papers and plainly too busy to bother with looking at drawings. He did not even glance up at Fred's approach. Fred fumbled in his big portfolio and pulled out a sketch. He held it toward the editor.

Wearily the editor reached for it, his head still bent over the papers on his desk. He was thinking crossly that he hadn't time today for would-be artists with no money and no talent. Then he saw the picture. His eyes widened. He felt as though he had been given an electric shock.

This, he realized, was the most remarkable work he had ever seen!

In later years that editor described what he saw in that first picture handed to him by Fred Remington.

The editor told people that:

Here was the real thing, the unspoiled native genius dealing with Mexican ponies, cowboys, cactus, lariats and sombreros. No stage heroes these; no pomaded hair and neatly tied cravats; these were the men of the real rodeo, parched in alkali dust, blinking out from barely opened eyelids under the furious rays of an Arizona sun. I had been there, and my innermost corpuscles vibrated at the truth before me.

But those words came later. Now the art editor only stared at the picture and felt that electric shock of discovery. Then he noticed the signature —Remington.

Still looking at the sketch, the editor said, "It's an odd coincidence, I had a classmate at Yale—"

Before he could finish, Remington's strong voice boomed, "Big!—Is it you?"

It was. Poultney Bigelow jumped up from his

desk. The two old friends pounded one another on the back and yelled their delight at this unexpected reunion. They made so much noise that people in an adjoining office rushed in, thinking a fight was going on.

Big introduced Fred.

Then from every drawer in his desk, Big began to pull stories and articles which needed the kind of illustrations that would interest Fred Remington. He searched out every piece that had anything in it about horses, cowboys, soldiers, or the West. He wanted all the work from Fred's drawing pen he could get.

Big gave Fred orders for dozens of pictures to be used in *Outing Magazine*.

At last a dazed but happy artist found himself on the street again. His shoulders were back, his head up. His neat blond mustache fairly bristled with excitement, and for so big a man he walked with airy steps. He had waited a long time for this day. He knew there was much hard work ahead before he achieved success. But Fred Remington was on his way at last!

10. Success Story

Now that he was earning money, Fred and Eva moved to a small apartment. They made the living room into a studio for Fred.

Up with the sun, he put in long hours with pen-and-ink, oil paints, and water colors. Late afternoons he and Eva went for walks through the city streets so that he could stretch his muscles and be ready to work again at night.

His style began to improve, for now he had time and quiet to polish his work. In the West, Fred had been always on the move or trying to work with constant interruptions of friends and outside activities. In the little apartment Eva saw to it

Remington drew from his memories of the West to
portray this Indian army scout signaling troops.

that nothing disturbed him when he sat before his easel or drawing board.

The long hours and hard work won for Fred a success beyond his dreams, and when success came to him it came with a rush. Within four years—well before his thirtieth birthday—he was famous.

During those years both the National Academy of Design and the American Water Color Society gave him major recognition by accepting his pictures to hang in their annual exhibitions. In 1887, the academy hung his painting "The Courier's Nap on the Trail," and the following year his "Return of a Blackfoot War Party" won both the Hallgarten and the Clarke prizes in the academy's annual exhibition. In 1887 the American Water Color Society accepted "The Flag of Truce in the Indian Wars" for exhibit, and in 1888 the impressive study of soldiers capturing a savage-faced renegade, "Arrest of a Blackfoot Murderer." In 1889 at the Paris (France) Exposition, Fred was awarded the Silver Medal for his work.

During these years, too, hundreds of Fred's drawings were published in the best magazines of the day. He illustrated important books, and his own first story was published—that story about "coursing" rabbits which he had written and illustrated on the sheep ranch back in Kansas.

Fred Remington—whom people had said would never amount to anything—became Frederic Remington, American artist.

Eva wrote a proud letter to friends. She said that Mr. Harper, whose *Harper's Weekly* had published Fred's first sketches, had taken Fred to lunch and told him he was the greatest artist in America!

Fred's love for the West remained strong. He longed to see it again and his chance came in the summer of 1888. *Century Magazine* assigned him to go to Arizona Territory where the Apaches were causing new trouble. Since there were few cameras in the West then, artists were often sent to interpret the news and illustrate it with sketches made on the spot.

Fred's assignment was to write and illustrate a series of articles about the army's efforts to control Geronimo and his tribesmen. They were attacking white settlements again. Fred joined a scouting party of the United States Tenth Cavalry, a crack regiment of black soldiers.

Once again he rode the sands and rocky mountain ridges of Arizona in blazing summer weather. It was so hot that the barrel of his carbine burned his hands. At every opportunity he got his sketchbook and drew the life he saw around him.

The troopers and their poor tired beasts did not look like the cavalry heroes in storybooks. They had been on too many hard marches.

He drew the ill-fed, hard-ridden cavalry horses with their bones showing sharply through their skins. The proud arch was gone from their necks, and their ears flapped almost like the ears of mules.

He drew the cavalrymen in their dusty boots and patched trousers, with unbuttoned coats and battered hats. Their faces were stubbled with three-day-old beards.

He drew these troopers as they looked in early morning when they hurried to obey the sergeant's command of "Catch your horses!" He drew them "saddling up," and on the long marches with the

In the West Remington
drew these black soldiers
of the Tenth Cavalry and
an Apache scout for his
articles in *Century*.

sun in their eyes, and in quick sharp battles with hostile tribesmen. He drew them as they gathered around a desert well, men and their horses in patient lines waiting their turns at the drinking trough. He drew the soldiers eating their scant meals, standing guard in pale moonlight, sleeping on the ground. He drew them wounded and he drew them slain.

He drew the miles of parched land dotted with cactus and mesquite, and once he drew a picture of himself riding behind the leader in a long cavalry column. The sketch showed him dressed in civilian khaki clothes and a tropical helmet.

When Fred returned home from that trip he did not need to describe it to Eva. She had only to look at his sketches to see it all. With the publication of the articles in *Century Magazine*, Fred began to win attention as a writer of vigorous prose.

An earlier assignment from that same magazine had brought Fred a lifelong friend who would one day become the twenty-sixth president of the United States.

Theodore Roosevelt was another New Yorker who, like Fred, had gone west in 1880. "Teddy" bought a cattle ranch in Dakota Territory. He learned the cowboy trade, went hunting and fishing, and wrote many magazine articles about his experiences. Fred had illustrated some of these articles for *Century Magazine*. Now, in the autumn of 1888, the articles were republished in a book called *Ranch Life and the Hunting Trail*, using the illustrations Fred had made—ninety-nine of them. The book was a great success. It established the reputations of Theodore Roosevelt as a writer and Frederic Remington as an illustrator.

That book helped Fred in another way, too. Ever since he had been illustrating he had wanted to make drawings for the great poem by Henry Wadsworth Longfellow called *The Song of Hiawatha*. It had never been published with illustrations.

It was a very long poem telling the story of an Indian boy who grew up to be a leader of his people in the days just before white men came to the

One of Frederic Remington's illustrations for the
great Longfellow poem, *The Song of Hiawatha*

New World. As a schoolboy Fred had memorized the lines about Hiawatha's childhood that began:

> By the shores of Gitche Gumee,
> By the shining Big-Sea-Water,
> Stood the wigwam of Nokomis,
> Daughter of the Moon, Nokomis.
> Dark behind it rose the forest—

The poem was filled with Indian legends and wisdom. It sang the music of winds and waters, and pictured the beauties of forests and meadows and dawns and sunsets.

It viewed the Indians sympathetically and so it struck a responsive chord in Fred's heart. He had sympathy for the red men. He knew them as individuals; some he admired and some he did not, just as with all people. He had sat in the te-pees of his friends and hunted with them on the plains. He wanted to illustrate the book-length poem that told the story of their race.

In the winter after the publication of *Ranch Life and the Hunting Trail*, Fred went to Boston

"The Santa Fe Trail"

"Fight for the Water Hole"

"*Bringing Home the New Cook*"

"Charge of the Rough Riders Up San Juan Hill"

to talk to a publisher about his ideas for the poem. The success of the Roosevelt book proved a help in selling these ideas to the book publishing house of Houghton, Mifflin and Company.

Fred was given the largest single assignment he had ever had. For this first illustrated edition of *The Song of Hiawatha* he was to make a total of 410 drawings and oil paintings.

He worked on them through the winter and spring. Then he and Eva went home to Canton to spend the summer.

It was not a holiday for Fred. While Eva and her friends fished and picnicked at Cranberry Lake nearby, Fred worked.

The *Plaindealer*, his father's old newspaper, printed an item about Fred: "Almost any morning will find him at work in his studio on State Street, surrounded by horses and attendants."

The studio was Uncle Horace Sackrider's old barn—that same barn where Fred had once "scalped" Badger!

The horses were on loan from friends and relatives, just as were the horses that Fred used to borrow in childhood days. The attendants were boys who were glad to hold halters, or sit astride horses, or model.

If a real horse wasn't available, Fred seated some youngster astride a wooden saw horse. He was good at improvising—when he didn't have the right "prop" he made something else do. Like most artists, he had a photographic memory. He could look at a shirtless boy on a sawhorse and remember exactly an Indian in breechclout on a racing pony.

So through the summer days Fred Remington worked in the old barn, illustrating the immortal story of Hiawatha.

11. Last of the Indian Wars

Fred and Eva stood on the front porch of their beautiful new home. They looked across a large lawn and could see Long Island Sound in the distance. The house was in New Rochelle, a pleasant town near New York City.

"Well, Missie—a home of our own at last!" Fred said triumphantly.

His wife smiled. Like Fred, she was proud of the big two-story mansion. It was furnished with fine antique furniture and with all the china and silver they needed for entertaining friends. Eva was a good hostess. Both she and Fred liked people. Their home was often filled with friends who came to enjoy "Endion's" hospitality. Endion was the name that the young Remingtons had given their house.

Fred had a stable out back with many horses, and he had added a wing to the house so that he could have the studio he'd always wanted.

The studio was a large room, twenty by forty feet, with a twenty-foot ceiling and a skylight. There was a huge brick fireplace and many windows. A double door led outside and was wide enough for two horses to walk through at the same time. Fred liked to bring his models right into the studio.

On the studio walls and shelves he had arranged all the articles he'd collected in the West and sent to his mother for safekeeping. There hung the fancy saddles and beaded bridles, the Indian war shields and lances, the moccasins and deerskin clothing. He needed these things so that every detail could be accurate in the pictures he painted. The articles almost covered the walls, yet he knew he would add more items in the years to come.

For Fred had begun to make yearly trips to the West to gather new material. He looked forward to these trips. Actually, Fred was like two different people. One was the eastern city man who lived in an elegant home and had many famous friends—a man who enjoyed fine food and fashionable clothes and all the things that money could buy. The other person was the western wanderer who delighted in living in the roughest, toughest spots in the West—a man who shared beans and coffee with cowpunchers over a campfire, and shared the dangers of the trail with army troopers on patrol.

Eva did not go with Fred on his western trips. She would not have enjoyed the hardships that to him seemed like fun. She was a small, delicate woman. Her "massive husband," as she called him, would have made almost three of her. It was no wonder he was large—a typical breakfast for him was six pork chops!

Fred and Eva were always happy together. Now they found added joy in this home of their own. As they looked from their porch across the broad lawn to the sparkling waters in the distance, their one regret was that they had no children.

Remington's drawing of the Oglala Sioux Ghost Dance
at Pine Ridge Agency, South Dakota

In the winter of 1890 the Remingtons were pre-
paring for their first Christmas in their new house.
Then word came that big trouble was brewing on
the Great Plains. Out in South Dakota the Sioux
Indians had adopted a strange new "religion"
called the Ghost Dance, and whites believed that
the Indians planned an uprising. *Harper's Weekly*
sent Fred west.

Once all of the Great Plains had been Indian
hunting ground. Vast herds of buffalo roamed the

grassy land and supplied almost every Indian need—meat, hides for tepees and robes, bones and horns and hooves for tools. With the westward migration of white settlers, the great herds were killed and the red men were pushed off their land.

By that winter of 1890, the northern tribes had been conquered by the army and put on government reservations. They had been promised food and clothing by the government as payment for their land that the whites had taken. However, they were seldom given enough of either. Often they were near starvation, and in the winter they were cold. Life on the reservations was bitterly hard for them, and they were reduced almost to prisoners.

Then hope came to the desperate people. From the Far West, a Nevada Paiute "medicine man" named Wovoka sent out word that he had visited the Great Spirit in heaven. He said the Great Spirit told him that a messiah was coming to save the Indians.

To hurry the messiah's coming, the Indians must wear magic "ghost shirts" through which, said Wovoka, no bullet would pass. They must dance a ghost dance and sing special songs. Then all the dead warriors would rise again. The white men would leave the country. The buffalo would come back.

Many Indians believed Wovoka. They made and wore the ghost shirts. They sang the songs and danced the dance.

"Soon now," they whispered to one another, "soon the messiah will come." They watched for their dead warriors to rise. They sent their young men out to scout for the first sign of the returning buffalo.

This was the situation that had frightened white people of the region. They believed that the aging Sioux chief, the great Sitting Bull, planned to lead the excited Indians against the whites. Men were sent to arrest him. The men handled the old chief so roughly that his followers grew angry and a gunfight broke out. Fourteen men were slain, including Sitting Bull.

Many outraged Sioux fled from the reservations and hid out in the Dakota Bad Lands. The army went after them. Fred Remington, as artist-reporter, joined a group of military scouts who were friendly Cheyenne Indians led by Lieutenant Edward W. Casey.

Some of the Cheyennes remembered Fred from earlier days. "What are you doing here?" asked old Wolf-Voice, a smile on his good brown face. High-Walking and Stump-Horn smiled their welcomes, too.

Fred was given a big, strawberry roan horse to ride.

It was below-zero weather when they set out for the Bad Lands—a rough, bleak land of steep trails and tall rock buttes. Under the cold blue winter sky it seemed to Fred as cruel and lonely a place as he had ever seen. That night they camped on a high mesa within sight of a Sioux camp. Hostile warriors, wearing war paint and ghost shirts, were on all sides. Sometimes a shot rang out, for the Indians were armed with Winchester rifles.

The lieutenant had been given orders not to fight the Sioux, but to powwow with them and try to get them to surrender peaceably. Despite the gunfire, Casey went alone to the Sioux camp. Fred and the others waited restlessly until he returned. He brought bad news—the Sioux would not surrender.

Other powwows followed, and late that night the Sioux did agree to let Casey send a wagon back to headquarters for more provisions so that the talks could continue. Nobody in the scout camp slept during those black hours. Any moment might bring the dreaded war whoop.

A wagon party of five men left for headquarters at dawn, among them Fred on his strawberry roan. Soon they realized that Sioux warriors were stationed everywhere, watching them. One false move could bring an attack. The wagon driver whipped his horses ahead and for several miles they made good speed.

Suddenly a group of Sioux appeared on the trail and stopped them. They must turn back, the Indians said. Fred felt a chill go down his spine at the hostile faces and threatening Winchesters.

Bang! Bang! Bang! All at once bullets were whistling about them.

Fred turned around and saw five fully-armed cowboys racing toward them. The punchers were coming to the rescue, whooping and firing guns as they came.

"Go back!" shouted the wagon driver. He was afraid that a "rescue" would start a real fight. The belligerent cowboys might easily antagonize the well-armed Indians hiding among the rocks and looking down from the high bluffs.

The cowboys came on, although they did stop shooting, and the Sioux who had stopped the wagon rode quickly away. Together the cowboys and the wagon men set off at a mad gallop down the trail. The wagon rattled and bumped, and the outfit made the last miles to headquarters in record-breaking time.

It had been a near thing. After so close a brush with trouble, Fred did not even mind the sleet that froze on his face as he slept that night in an army camp out of range of Sioux guns.

Fighting did break out between red and white men a few days later. At Wounded Knee Creek several hundred Sioux were wiped out by the

"The Opening of the Fight at Wounded Knee"

United States Seventh Cavalry. It was the last Indian battle fought on the Great Plains.

Fred was not at Wounded Knee, but he talked to many survivors and drew the scenes they described.

So ended the red men's hope that Wovoka's prophecies would come true. Frederic Remington, on the scene, sketched it all. His were the only

116

on-the-spot illustrations of the last days of the Indian wars. They were important pictorial documents of a chapter in American history, and they brought him new praise.

Years later Fred made another drawing—a poignant picture that expressed something of how he felt about the tragedy of the conquered red men. He called it "Twilight of the Indian."

It showed a young Indian of proud and noble bearing, plowing a fenced field. While his two bony horses rest, he stands staring off into a far vista of open plains. Once he would have been a hunter and warrior, free as the winds that ripple the prairie grass. Now he grips plow handles, his feet walk a furrow, and on his face is a look of great longing for a time that will never return.

12. Beauty in Bronze

Poultney Bigelow wanted Fred to go to Europe and Africa with him where they could visit the great art museums. However, Fred had little interest in European art. "No," he said.

"We can visit the great horse farms of the continent," Big pointed out.

"Yes!" said Fred.

They visited Kaiser Wilhelm's famous stud farms in Germany. They saw the cavalry horses of France, the well-trained mounts of Russian cossacks, and the splendid Arabian steeds of North Africa. In London Fred spent much time at Buffalo Bill's Wild West Show, which was on tour there.

His friendship with the buffalo hunter and showman—whose real name was Colonel William F. Cody—dated back to Fred's early days in the West.

Fred and Big visited art galleries, and many of the antique wonders of the Old World. Fred sketched and wrote articles, but he did not enjoy the trip. When he was back home again, he said:

> I shall not try Europe again. I am not built right. I hate parks—collars—cuffs —foreign languages—cut-and-dried stuff. . . . I am going to do *America—* it's new—it's to my taste. . . . I am 240 pounds and feel bully . . . nothing can stop me but an incurable disease.

He continued to "do" America. One big project was illustrating a book by the American historian Francis Parkman.

Long before Fred was born, Parkman had made a trip to Wyoming where he lived with and studied the Sioux Indians. He described that visit in a volume called *The Oregon Trail*, which soon became a classic in American literature. Now the famous book was to be published in a new edition. The aging historian was delighted to have Frederic Remington do the illustrations.

"Your rendering of Western life is superior to any other artist," he wrote Fred. "You have seen so much and observed so closely that you have no rival."

With the publication of the two classic books, *The Song of Hiawatha* and *The Oregon Trail*, the name of Frederic Remington became recognized as that of the greatest illustrator in the nation.

Fred was also working seriously with oil painting. He was teaching himself and progress was slow, but he knew he was learning. The more he worked with colors, the more they excited him.

"I am sufficiently idiotic to have a *color sense* and I am going to go *loco* for two months," he told friends when he was planning a trip into the colorful western desert.

A milestone in his career, as it is for any artist, was his first art exhibit. For years his work had been hung in various art exhibitions, but that was not the same as having a show entirely his own. He exhibited one hundred drawings and paintings, and sold ninety-six of them. Another milestone was the publication of his first book, *Pony Tracks*. It was a collection of magazine stories and articles he had written about the West.

Busy as he was, Fred found time to enjoy his New Rochelle home. Almost every evening friends came to Endion for dinner, or for good talk in Fred's studio. "Come up here and smoke my cigars and drink my rum and eat my grub and you're always welcome," he told friends. With his good neighbor, the playwright Augustus Thomas, he skated and hiked in the winter, and in summer the two swam, bicycled, and played tennis together.

"I don't like the fuss and feathers of society," Fred said, although that did not stop him from taking Eva to the dances and theatres that she loved. One reason he did not like "society" was that he was shy around most women except Eva. He seldom put a woman in his pictures, and when he did he often removed her.

"I washed her out," he would say cheerfully.

He was a "man's man"—a man "with the bark still on," as people said. His art was "hard as nails." He had lived too long during the formative years of his youth among the rough, tough men of the Old West. He hadn't learned to enjoy the "cards and custards" of social life. The only parties he liked were the ones that he and Eva held at Endion.

Although his shyness sometimes made him seem gruff to women, his friends knew that nobody had greater good humor and sympathy for people than Fred Remington. He was a good listener and a good laugher. His humor was western, fresh, and wholesome. He usually whistled or sang as he worked at his easel, and his friendships were long-lasting. When Fred made a friend, it was for life.

One summer day the New York City sculptor, Frederic W. Ruckstull, came to New Rochelle and set up a tent on a vacant lot near Fred's place. He began to construct a clay model for a large equestrian statue that was to stand in front of the Pennsylvania State Capitol at Harrisburg.

Fred sauntered down to the tent to meet the newcomer. He had never before seen sculpture in the making. He stood with legs apart, his fists jammed into his pockets, and watched in fascination as the sculptor worked deftly on the form.

"Ever try modeling?" Ruckstull asked.

"No," Fred replied. "But if I did, I'd model a horse. A Western horse—a real wild bronco."

"Put a rider on him," advised the sculptor. "It makes for a more interesting composition."

Every day for the two months that Ruckstull worked in New Rochelle, Fred visited the tent.

One afternoon the following winter, Augustus Thomas sat in Fred's studio watching him illustrate a story by Owen Wister. Wister was a novelist of western subjects and a friend of Fred's.

Fred was working without models that day. He was drawing on a big cardboard twenty-four by thirty inches. Later the drawing would be reduced by photographic process to the size needed for a page. Thomas followed his friend's work as Fred made his first marks with charcoal. The outline began to show a cowboy "shooting up" a barroom.

The cowboy stood in the front of the picture, shooting toward the back with its bar and panicked customers. But the cowboy's big figure blocked out much of the rear detail.

Fred stepped back a few paces and studied his work. Then with one swipe he dusted off the drawing and redrew it, completely reversing the scene. This time the cowboy stood to the rear, shooting toward the front where the bar and the victims were now clearly shown.

As Augustus Thomas watched, he realized that Fred could just as easily have put his cowboy to either side of the barroom.

"You're not an illustrator so much as you're a sculptor," Thomas told Fred. "You don't see your figures on one side or the other—your mind goes all around them."

Not long afterward, Fred bought a set of tools. Fred began making his first statue—a twenty-two-inch figure of a cowboy riding a bucking bronco. He named it "The Bronco Buster."

It was like Fred that his first attempt at sculpture should be such a difficult subject—a wildly

Although "The Bronco Buster" was Remington's first attempt at sculpture, it became the best-known work of its kind by an American artist.

rearing horse standing on its hind legs in a furious effort to buck off its cowboy rider.

An experienced sculptor would have had trouble with that subject. Fred had trouble too, but at last he succeeded in giving his composition the balance and grace it needed.

"The Bronco Buster" was cast in bronze under a copyright date of October 1, 1895—Fred's thirty-fourth birthday. By chance, and the good advice of a friend, he had tried his hand at a new art form and discovered another aspect of his genius.

In his lifetime Fred made a total of twenty-five bronzes. All were superb, but "The Bronco Buster" became the best-known work of its kind by any American artist. More than 300 castings were made and sold before the mold was destroyed.

Fred wrote Owen Wister about his new-found love for sculpture. "I always had a feeling for mud," he joked. He said that "mud" didn't decay, moths wouldn't eat it, and neither time nor rust could blacken it.

Triumphantly he told his friend, "They are writing editorials out West about the Buster!"

13. The Charge
at San Juan Hill

On a February morning in 1898, the telephone rang at Endion. When Fred answered, he heard Augustus Thomas' excited voice.

"The *Maine* has been blown up and sunk in Havana Harbor!" Thomas cried.

"Ring off!" shouted Fred. Immediately he called his publishers in New York City. The *Maine* was an American battleship. It had been sent to the Cuban harbor during a dispute between the United States and Spain because of Spanish misrule of Cuba. Fred knew that the sinking of the ship by Spaniards might well mean war.

During the next weeks he made preparations to go to Cuba. If war came, he was to do stories and pictures for *Harper's Weekly* and for a New York newspaper. The war came.

Fred hit the Cuban beachhead with the United States Sixth Cavalry on the first afternoon of the Spanish-American War on Cuban soil. Sketching and interviewing people, he moved about the countryside for days.

Finally he made his way through steaming jungle heat to San Juan Hill, a Spanish stronghold on the way to the city of Santiago. There he witnessed one of the most decisive battles of the war.

Later he wrote in his articles how he came in view of the hill. "I went down the creek. . . . hunting for our line. Bullets cut and clicked around me, and a sharpshooter nearly did me. I ran quickly across a space. 'Wheet' came a Mauser, and it was right next to my ear, and two more. I dropped in the tall guinea-grass, and crawled to some soldiers hidden under a mango tree."

He had lost his sketchbook in that mad scramble, but he didn't crawl back to get it. He had too much respect for Spanish shooting.

This picture of cavalrymen attacking a Spanish position was painted from on-the-scene sketches.

Fred watched the assault on the hill, and finally saw blue-coated American soldiers on the hilltop.

"Only a handful of men got to the top, where they broke out a flag and cheered," he wrote. "'Cheer' is the right word for that sound. You have got to hear it once where it means so much, and ever after you will thrill when Americans make that noise."

Later, Fred climbed up the hill and stood with American troops during a desperate counterattack by the enemy.

For days he'd had nothing to eat but crackers and muddy water. Fever struck him down when he got back to camp. He lay on the ground in the terrible heat and watched with fever-dulled eyes as reinforcements moved toward the front.

When he tried to get up and join them, he fell weakly to the ground again. With other sick and wounded he was returned home.

Out of that experience Fred made some important pictures, and one had a far-reaching effect.

* He called it "Charge of the Rough Riders Up San Juan Hill." It shows Fred's good friend Lt. Colonel Theodore Roosevelt, leading his Rough Rider troops in a gallant charge up the hill. Some people said that this picture, portraying "Teddy" Roosevelt as a hero, helped Roosevelt later to become president of the United States.

When the Rough Riders disbanded after the war, they gave their leader a parting gift. It was a bronze statue of "The Bronco Buster."

Roosevelt wrote Fred: "It was the most appropriate gift the Regiment could have given . . ."

Fred wrote back telling his friend: "I am very proud that the Rough Riders have put their brand on my Bronco Buster."

* In color on page 104

14. An Artist's Life

Shortly after the war the Remingtons bought a summer home. It was an island of five acres in Chippewa Bay on the St. Lawrence River—a beautiful place of white rocks and green pines.

"We can have a canoe," Fred told Eva happily. "Canoeing is the best exercise in the world."

"Ingleneuk," as they called the island, became a little kingdom to the couple. For ten years they spent part of each summer there. In the evenings Fred paddled his canoe out upon the river and watched the setting sun color the waters pink and gold.

"Seems as if I *must* paint them," he told his

friend and neighbor, Edwin Wildman, who lived beside the water. "Seems as though they'd never be so beautiful again. But people won't stand for my painting sunsets." Fred whooped with laughter at the thought of what people would say. "They've got me pigeon-holed in their minds, you see. Want horses, cowboys, out-West things—won't believe me if I paint anything else."

But for himself, sometimes at a summer's end he'd paint a picture of his boathouse or the blue water lapping the white shore.

"Got to take some of the light and water home with me to look at this winter," he explained.

Fred found the island an especially good place to write. Much of his writing was about the West. Among his books were *Crooked Trails*, *Stories of War and Peace*, and *The Way of an Indian*.

He wrote about hunting and fishing, too, for he made many trips to forests and streams. He hunted moose in Canada and the piglike peccary in Mexico. He trailed grizzly bears in the Rocky Mountains and fished for tarpon in Florida waters. He went after caribou, and blue quail, and trout, and antelope. He sketched and painted and wrote about all of it.

He wrote about horses, not only western horses but those of the sporting world—polo ponies, hunters, racers, trotters. He wrote about training horses.

"You can teach a horse anything, but you can't unteach him," Fred said.

He said that when he died the only epitaph he wanted carved on his tombstone was: "He Knew the Horse." One of the darker hours of Fred's life came when he realized that he had grown too heavy to ride anymore.

Almost as if to compensate for the loss of horseback riding, Fred's oil paintings began to win serious attention.

Some of his paintings were published as full-color, double-page spreads in *Collier's Weekly*, a leading magazine. Some were reproduced in color prints suitable for framing, and they sold widely to the public. Some were hung in national art exhibitions and in Fred's one-man shows in art galleries.

A detail from "A Dash for Timber"

Among the paintings that won instant popularity was "Caught in the Circle." It appeared in *Collier's* in 1901, and showed a typical struggle to the death on the plains. Four frontiersmen are making a desperate stand against hostile Indians who ride in circles around them. The men's horses lie wounded or dead; soon the men too will be slain.

*   "Fight for the Water Hole" has a similar theme. This time a few grim-faced frontiersmen crouch on the hot sand and shoot at circling Indians. Behind them is a small blue pool of water where the party had stopped to water the drooping horses and fill canteens. Precious water holes were far apart on the dry southwestern desert, and Indians often lay in wait nearby to ambush travelers.

*   "The Emigrants" was based on a true incident told to Fred by the only survivor. The painting shows a wagon train attacked at a river crossing by war-feathered braves. A boy of fourteen stands knee-deep in the water beside his ox team and strikes out with a long pole at an Indian who rides

* These paintings in color on pages 51 and 102

toward him with poised lance. It is a scene painted in soft shades of blue and brown—blue water and sky and distant hills, yellow browns of prairie and red browns of animals and men.

In the actual fight, wagons and people were destroyed, and the boy was scalped and left for dead. Somehow he survived. When he described his ordeal to Fred, the artist painted a picture that told the whole story without need for a word.

One of Fred's most popular paintings was "A Dash for Timber." It portrays a small group of cavalrymen firing back at a band of pursuing * Indians. Another success was "Downing the Nigh Leader," which shows red warriors racing beside a six-horse stagecoach as they send arrows into the horse ranks.

People pointed out that Frederic Remington's work had two main themes, or motifs: Struggle and The Horse.

The struggle was not always between man and man. Often it was between man and animals—a buffalo hunt, a cattle stampede, a wild-eyed bronc. Or it might be the struggle of man against the

* In color on page 52

dangers of nature—a prairie fire, a great storm, the swift currents of a dangerous river.

There are quieter pictures, too. Such is "Evening on a Canadian Lake," a painting of calm beauty which depicts two men in a canoe at twilight drifting on lavender and purple waters. * "Bringing Home the New Cook" is a jolly scene of whooping cowboys on prancing horses as they escort the new—and, they hope, good!—cook to the cattle ranch. Fred's oils, like his drawings, cover every aspect of western life: "Coming and Going of the Pony Express," "The Old Stage-* coach of the Plains," "On the Oregon Trail," "The Santa Fe Trail," "Protecting the Wagon Train," "The Round-Up," "Riding Herd in Winter," and many more. Each is story and history combined.

Some of Fred's most popular paintings were of animals, such as the poignant night scene, "The Last March," in which wolves yelp and snap at the heels of a lone, lost horse. His saddle is empty; somewhere back on the trail his rider lies dead. Soon the wolves will grow bold enough to attack him. In the meantime the horse plods wearily on,

* These paintings in color on pages 101 and 103

and the desert stars look down on his last lonely march.

Painting, sculpturing, writing—it seemed that Fred was never idle a moment.

One summer at Ingleneuk he decided to write a novel. He put aside all other work and began a romance set in the West.

The title is *John Ermine of the Yellowstone*, and it tells a tragic story of a handsome, golden-haired white boy who was raised by an Indian trapper. When he grew to manhood he became a United States Army scout and had to lead white men against his foster parents, the Sioux. Worse yet for John, he fell in love with the army major's pretty daughter, but the major disapproved.

When it was published, the novel was successful and was made into a stage play. But Fred didn't know about that during the Ingleneuk summer. He only knew that writing a novel was very hard for him, especially the love scenes. He was glad to finish the book one sunny afternoon, and he lost no time getting out on the river in his beloved canoe.

He pulled up at Edwin Wildman's dock and shouted for Ed.

When Ed came to the dock, Fred said, "I've coined two words today—the sweetest ones in the English language."

"What are they?" Ed wanted to know.

"Come close," Fred said. "Bend low. I want to whisper them to you."

Ed bent low over the water.

Suddenly the big man in the canoe whooped, "T-H-E E-N-D."

Then he paddled merrily away.

15. End of the Trail

Frederic Remington had crusaded to make a place in the art world for "out-West things." His big breakthrough came when the Metropolitan Museum of Art in New York City bought four of his bronzes. It was public recognition of his work as true art.

Now his fame rocketed.

His one-man exhibit at The Knoedler Galleries in 1908 was the most successful he'd ever had. Art critics welcomed him to "the ranks of the old masters" for such paintings as "With the Eye of the Mind" and "Stampeded by Lightning."

The first is an interpretative picture of the awe with which three mounted Indians regard a cloud apparition in the sky. "Stampeded by Lightning" depicts a rain-drenched cowboy as he races his horse through the night trying to stop a stampede of panicked cattle.

Fred had painted the stampede scene many times before, but was dissatisfied with the pictures and burned them. Now he was willing to let this one stand.

He burned many of his paintings for he was seldom satisfied with his work. In that year of

"Stampeded by Lightning"

1908 he wrote in his diary: "A man named Fisher wants to sell my early painting, 'The Missionary.' Thus my early crimes come back to haunt me. I am helpless. I would buy them all if I were able and burn them." Then the diary listed a number of paintings that he had burned that day.

On another occasion he told his diary: "Burned every old canvas in the house today—out on the snow. About 75 paintings."

Fred wanted every detail to be right in his pictures. Once he spent days trying to get the exact effect of raindrops bouncing on the quiet surface of a pool.

His sure eye for accuracy sometimes aroused controversy. When he painted horses running with all four feet off the ground, there were people who said that was against the nature of horses. Then high-speed photography proved that horses sometimes *do* run with all four hooves in the air at once.

Fred was equally critical of the work of other artists if he suspected they had faked details, or if their technique seemed careless to him. Once, looking as some paintings in a exhibition, he exploded: "I have two aunts who can *knit* better pictures than those!"

The success of his great 1908 show delighted him. With glee he confided to his diary: "My show closes at Knoedler's tonight. It was a triumph. I have landed among the painters, and well up too."

Now people wondered if Fred could ever repeat such a success. He did, in his 1909 exhibit.

Such crowds attended that the exhibition room was not large enough to hold them. "No American artist interests the American people more than Remington does, and none is really better worth going to see," said one New York newspaper.

A critic wrote: "Remington is one of the few men in this country who has created new conditions in our art, and must be reckoned with as one of the revolutionary figures in our art history."

Another said: "Remington's work is splendid in its technique, epic in its imaginative qualities, and historically important. . . . American history, so far as it is concerned with the plains and the Indians, will be made more vivid to the youths of the future through Remington's canvasses and drawings, than through printed pages, no matter who the author."

Among the large canvasses were several that critics called the best he had ever done. His earlier tendency to use harsh, sometimes glaring colors had disappeared. He had begun to capture the sunlight of the plains, and the silver mystery of moonlight. "The Love Call," which portrayed an Indian wooer blowing his flute at the foot of a tree in the enchanted moonlight, was called "a triumph of beautiful characterization."

The critics agreed that Frederic Remington's exhibit had proved his genius. No one could know that it would be his last show.

That same year Fred and Eva moved to Ridgefield, Connecticut. They built a large house on ten acres there, with Fred overseeing every detail. Again there was a big studio and a big stable. Since Fred could no longer ride, there were no horses except one small pinto pony. He was everybody's pet. Fred called the Ridgefield place "The One Hoss Farm." Fred liked his "farm" so much that his friends had trouble getting him to parties, and when he did go to a party he left it early.

"Fred's going home to milk the cows," his friends laughed.

At Ridgefield Fred produced his finest bronze, "Stampede."

Like his pictures, his sculptures told the story of the West. Most of the sculptures represented violent scenes, with horses and men caught at peak action or facing grave danger.

Among these were "The Rattlesnake" which shows a horse shying at a snake in the path and almost unseating his rider. "The Norther" portrays a man on horseback in a snowstorm, with a strong wind blowing from the rear and the man and horse almost frozen. "The Wicked Pony" depicts a true incident in which a bronco threw and killed his rider.

"The Wounded Bunkie" is an ambitious—and typical—sculpture. One critic said it shows

Remington sculpting "The Buffalo Horse" in his studio in Ridgefield, Connecticut

"Remington's complete mastery of the nature and anatomy of the horse. . . . The action is superb . . . the whole group in the most natural manner possible." The sculpture is of two horses with cavalry riders at full gallop and the group is supported only by one hind leg of one horse and a foreleg of the other. One trooper is wounded and is kept from falling by an arm of his companion who is riding alongside.

Fred made great plans at Ridgefield for future work. One of the most important to him was his dream of doing the figure of an Indian in heroic size. He envisioned this sculpture placed upon Staten Island where the island extends farthest out into the Atlantic Ocean.

It would be a monument to the first inhabitants of the American continent, and on its island location it would be the first thing that visitors to the United States would see from far out at sea. The red man would stand like a welcoming host to this land of his ancestors. The statue would be Fred Remington's tribute to the American Indian.

He did not have a chance to do it.

A few days before Christmas he became ill. Fred was unused to illness, so he went about his work without realizing the seriousness of his condition. When he grew worse and finally asked for medical help, it was too late. After an emergency operation for appendicitis, he died on December 26, 1909. He was only forty-eight years old. He was buried in Canton, where he had been born.

When art people totaled up the work that Fred

had done in his too-short life, they were amazed at how much he had accomplished. They said he had done more than three men might do.

His name was on almost 2,800 paintings and drawings, and twenty-five bronzes. His illustrations had appeared in forty-one different periodicals, and in 142 books in addition to 13 books he had written himself.

Fred had always said, "I paint for boys from ten to seventy." However, men of authority said he painted for history. Among them was Theodore Roosevelt, who had lived in the Old West himself. When he was president, he said of Fred:

> He has portrayed a most characteristic and yet vanishing type of American life. The soldier, the cowboy and rancher, the Indian, the horses and the cattle of the Plains, will live in his pictures and his bronzes, I verily believe, for all time.

Today his art is exhibited in some of the world's

greatest museums, his books are republished in new editions, and the name of Frederic Remington has become a symbol of the Old American West.

Not long ago two friends stood before a Remington painting of Indians on the warpath.

"Be quiet," said the older man.

The younger man listened for a moment. "I don't hear anything," he said.

"Sh-h! Can't you hear the hoofbeats of those Indian ponies?" whispered his friend.

When we stand before a Remington painting we can indeed feel the hot sunshine or the bitter winds, smell the gunsmoke, hear the shouts of struggling men and the hoofbeats of running ponies. True, the picture is only a thing of paint and canvas, but the hand of genius gave it a life of its own.

Index

Apache Indians, 75, 76, 77, 78, 94
"The Apache War: Indian Scouts on Geronimo's Trail," 86, 87 (pic)
Arizona, 58, 60, 75, 78, 94, 95
"Arrest of a Blackfoot Murderer," 93

Badger, 9, 13, 14, 15, 16, 105
Bigelow, Poultney, 30, 31, 33, 35, 89, 90, 118, 119
"Boots and Saddles," 58
"Bringing Home the New Cook," 103 (color pic), 137
"The Bronco Buster," 124, 125 (pic), 126, 130
"A Bucking Bronco," 1 (pic)

Camp, Robert, 63, 64, 65
Casey, Edward W., 113, 114
Caten, Eva Adele. *See* Remington, Eva Caten
Caten, Lawton, 37, 39
"Caught in the Circle," 135
Century Magazine, 94, 97, 98
"Ceremony of the Scalps," 49 (color pic)
"The Charge," 58
"Charge of the Rough Riders Up San Juan Hill," 104 (color pic), 130
"A Cheyenne Agency Policeman," 57
Collier's Weekly, 133, 135
Comanches, 67, 69
"Coming and Going of the Pony Express," 137

"The Courier's Nap on the Trail," 93
"Coursing Rabbits on the Plains," 68, 94
Cowboys, 54 (pic), 59 (pic at top)
"Cowboys of Arizona," 60
"Cowboys Coming to Town for Christmas," 42 (pic)
Crooked Trails, 32
"A Crow Scout," 57

Dakota Territories, 20, 48, 98, 110, 112
"A Dash for Timber," 134 (pic), 136
de Thulstrup, T., 73
"Downing the Nigh Leader," 52 (color pic), 136

"Ejecting an Oklahoma Boomer," 73
"The Emigrants," 51 (color pic), 135
Endion, 107-108, 121, 122, 127
"Evening on a Canadian Lake," 137

"The Faun," 30, 31, 35
"Fight for the Water Hole," 102 (color pic), 135
"The Flag of Truce in the Indian Wars," 93

Geronimo, 75, 86, 94

Harper, J. Henry, 86, 94
Harper's Weekly, 60, 73, 86, 94, 110, 128

150

Highland Military Academy, 24, 26, 29

"In from the Night Herd," 56 (pic), 57
"Indian Reservation Horse Race," 80 (pic)
Ingleneuk, 131, 138

John Ermine of the Yellowstone, 138

"A Kiowa Buck," 57
Knoedler Galleries, 140, 143

"The Last March," 137
"The Love Call," 144

Missie. *See* Remington, Eva Caten
"The Missionary," 142
Montana Territory, 20, 38, 39, 40-41, 44, 45, 46, 48, 53, 54, 58, 81

National Academy of Design, 93
"Night Halt of Cavalry," 58
"The Norther," 145

"The Old Stagecoach of the Plains," 137
"An Old Time Plains Fight," 50 (color pic)
"On the Oregon Trail," 137
The Oregon Trail, 120
Outing Magazine, 68, 88

Parkman, Francis, 119
Pony Tracks, 121

"Protecting the Wagon Train," 137
"The Pursuit," 58

Ranch Life and the Hunting Trail, 98, 100
"The Rattlesnake," 145
Remington, Clara (mother), 11, 12, 15, 16, 17, 21, 22, 25, 30, 33, 34, 35, 36, 38, 60, 61, 63, 74
Remington, Eva Caten, 36, 37, 38, 61, 63, 71, 72, (pic), 74, 82, 85, 91, 94, 97, 105, 107, 109, 121, 122, 131, 144
Remington, Frederic Sackrider childhood of, 6 (pic), 7-29, 18 (pic)
death of, 147
education of, 7-10, 24-29, 28 (pic), 30-34, 32 (pic), 85-86
and European travels, 118-119
and horses, 74, 80, 81, 133, 136, 142, 146
and illustrating, 23 (pic), 94, 98, 99 (pic), 100-105, 119-120, 148
and Kansas ranch, 63-68, 66 (pic), 69 (pic)
marriage of, 71
in New York City, 84-94 97-100
and painting, 27, 55-57, 58, 68, 85-86, 93, 120-121, 130, 132, 133-138, 140-144, 148, 149

at San Carlos Reservation,
  77-79
and sculpting, 123-126, 130,
  140, 145-147, 146 (pic),
  148
and Spanish-American War,
  127-130, 129 (pic)
in the West, 40-61, 62-71,
  73-84, 78 (pic), 95-98,
  113-117
and writing, 29, 68-70, 121,
  132, 133, 138, 148
Remington, Samuel
  (grandfather), 17
Remington, Seth (father), 11,
  12 (pic), 14, 15, 16, 17,
  20, 21, 22, 23, 24, 30, 33,
  34, 35, 38
"A Reservation Comanche,"
  57
"Return of a Blackfoot War
  Party," 93
Ridgefield, Conn., 144-145,
  147
"Riding Herd in Winter," 137
Rocky Mountains, 20, 44, 132
Rogers, W. A., 60-61
Roosevelt, Theodore, 98, 105,
  130, 148
"The Round Up," 137
Ruckstull, Frederic W., 122,
  123

Sackrider, Henry L.
  (grandfather), 17
Sackrider, Horace (uncle), 12,
  105
St. Lawrence Plaindealer, 11,
  19, 105

San Juan Hill, 127, 128, 130
"The Santa Fe Trail," 101
  (color pic), 137
"A Scout Signaling the Main
  Column," 92 (pic)
Sioux Ghost Dance, 110
  (pic), 110-112
Sioux Indians, 110, 112, 113,
  114, 115, 119, 138
The Song of Hiawatha,
  98-100, 99 (pic), 105,
  106, 120
"Stampede," 145
"Stampeded by Lightning,"
  140, 141 (pic)
Stories of War and Peace, 132

Terra Cotta, 62, 63, 65, 67,
  68, 74
Thomas, Augustus, 123, 124,
  127
Turner, Scott, 26, 27, 29
"Twilight of the Indian," 117

The Way of an Indian, 132
"The Wicked Pony," 145
Wilder, Julian, 26, 27
"With the Eye of the Mind,"
  140
"The Wounded Bunkie," 145
Wounded Knee Creek, 115,
  116 (pic)
Wovoka, 111, 112, 116

Yale College, 30, 32, 34, 35,
  38, 53, 63, 64, 85, 89
Yale Courant, 33
"A Yuma Apache," 57